Why Scotland Should Become An Independent Country

By
James Hosie

1

Self-Governance and Policy Autonomy in an Independent Scotland:

One compelling argument in favor of Scottish independence revolves around the concept of self-governance. Independence provides Scotland with the opportunity to exert full control over its domestic and foreign policies, shaping the nation's destiny according to its own unique priorities and aspirations.

1. Domestic Policy Determination:
With self-governance, Scotland gains the authority to formulate and implement policies that directly address its specific economic, social,

and cultural needs. This autonomy empowers the Scottish government to tailor legislation, social welfare programs, and economic strategies to best serve the interests of its citizens.

2. Cultural Identity Preservation:
Independence allows for the preservation and promotion of Scotland's distinctive cultural identity. The freedom to make decisions regarding language, education, and cultural initiatives enables the nation to safeguard and celebrate its rich heritage.

3. Economic Control and Resource Management:
One of the driving forces behind self-governance is the desire for increased economic control. Independence provides Scotland with the ability to

manage its own resources, including
North Sea oil, and formulate economic
policies that align with its specific
economic goals.

**4. Responsive Crisis
Management:**
An independent Scotland would be
better positioned to respond rapidly
and effectively to domestic crises.
With full control over policies, the
government can enact targeted
measures in times of economic
downturns, public health emergencies,
or other challenges.

**5. Social Policies Aligned with
Values:**
Self-governance enables the crafting of
social policies that align closely with
Scottish values and priorities. This may
include initiatives related to healthcare,

education, social welfare, and other aspects that resonate with the ethos of the Scottish population.

6. Democratic Representation: Independence enhances the democratic representation of the Scottish people. With a government solely accountable to the Scottish electorate, decision-making becomes more directly tied to the preferences and aspirations of the citizens.

7. Foreign Policy Independence: On the international stage, an independent Scotland can establish its own foreign policies, forging diplomatic relationships based on its unique interests and values. This includes participation in international organizations and the ability to engage with global issues independently.

8. Responsive Legal System:
Full control over the legal system allows Scotland to adapt and shape its laws to reflect evolving societal norms and values. This ensures a legal framework that resonates with the people it governs.

9. Innovation and Technology Strategies:
Independence opens avenues for tailored innovation and technology strategies. Scotland can pursue policies that foster research, development, and technological advancements aligned with its economic goals and societal needs.

10. Flexibility in Environmental Policies:

With self-governance, Scotland can implement environmentally sustainable policies tailored to its unique ecosystems and landscapes. This includes strategies for conservation, renewable energy adoption, and climate change mitigation.

In summary, the pursuit of self-governance through independence offers Scotland the prospect of a more responsive and tailored governance structure, allowing the nation to navigate its own path and address the challenges and opportunities specific to its context.

2

Preserving and Promoting Scottish Cultural Identity through Independence:

The call for Scottish independence resonates strongly with the aspiration to safeguard and celebrate the rich tapestry of Scottish cultural identity. Independence provides a unique opportunity to preserve, revitalize, and promote the distinctive elements that define Scotland's historical, linguistic, and artistic heritage.

1. Language and Linguistic Autonomy:
Independence empowers Scotland to protect and nurture its linguistic diversity. With full control over language policies, the Scottish government can actively support the use and preservation of languages such as Scots and Scottish Gaelic, reinforcing a sense of linguistic identity and cultural continuity.

2. Educational Empowerment:
An independent Scotland can design an educational curriculum that places a premium on Scottish history, literature, and cultural achievements. This ensures that future generations are well-versed in the unique contributions of Scotland to the world, fostering a strong cultural identity from an early age.

3. Cultural Heritage Protection:
Independence provides the means to enact policies that safeguard Scotland's cultural heritage, including historical landmarks, traditions, and artifacts. This protection becomes vital in maintaining a tangible link to the past and fostering a sense of pride and continuity.

4. Arts and Creative Industries:
Cultural independence allows for the flourishing of Scotland's arts and creative industries. With control over cultural funding and promotion, the nation can invest in and elevate its musicians, artists, writers, and filmmakers, both domestically and on the global stage.

5. Festivals and Celebrations:
An independent Scotland can amplify the significance of traditional festivals and celebrations, reinforcing their cultural importance. Events like Hogmanay, Burns Night, and Highland Games can be elevated, attracting international attention while fostering a sense of unity and pride among the Scottish people.

6. Cultural Diplomacy:

Independence enables Scotland to engage in cultural diplomacy independently. The nation can actively promote its cultural exports, establish cultural exchange programs, and participate in international forums, strengthening global awareness and appreciation of Scottish heritage.

7. Media Representation:
Full control over media policies allows an independent Scotland to shape how its culture is represented in the media. This includes supporting Scottish content creators, fostering diverse narratives, and ensuring that the media landscape reflects the richness and diversity of Scottish identity.

8. Heritage Tourism:
Independence facilitates the development of a tailored tourism

strategy that highlights Scotland's cultural heritage. Preserving and promoting historical sites, museums, and cultural events can attract tourists interested in experiencing the unique aspects of Scottish identity.

9. Cultural Inclusivity:
Independence provides the platform to promote cultural inclusivity, acknowledging the diversity within the Scottish identity. This may involve recognizing and celebrating the contributions of various ethnic, religious, and immigrant communities to Scotland's cultural mosaic.

10. Creative Freedom and Expression:
Cultural independence ensures that Scottish artists and creators have the creative freedom to explore and

express the nuances of their identity without external constraints. This freedom is fundamental in fostering a vibrant and evolving cultural landscape.

In conclusion, independence offers Scotland the agency to actively nurture, protect, and project its cultural identity on the global stage. By doing so, it not only preserves the past but also lays the foundation for a dynamic and flourishing cultural legacy for generations to come.

3

Economic Empowerment through Independence: Gaining Control Over Policies and Resources in Scotland

The pursuit of Scottish independence is often underpinned by the desire to attain greater economic control, allowing the nation to tailor its policies and efficiently manage its resources. This economic empowerment is seen as a pathway to fostering sustainable growth, responding to specific challenges, and capitalizing on Scotland's unique economic strengths.

1. Resource Management: Independence provides Scotland with direct control over its abundant natural resources, including North Sea oil and renewable energy sources. This control enables strategic, sustainable management of these resources for the benefit of the Scottish economy.

2. Fiscal Policy Autonomy:

An independent Scotland gains the power to set and adjust its fiscal policies according to its economic needs. This includes the ability to determine tax rates, manage public spending, and implement economic stimuli tailored to the unique economic landscape of Scotland.

3. Trade and Investment Strategies:
Independence allows for the formulation of independent trade and investment strategies. Scotland can negotiate trade agreements that align with its economic priorities, fostering international partnerships that benefit specific sectors and industries.

4. Economic Diversification:
With increased control, Scotland can actively pursue economic

diversification strategies, reducing dependence on specific industries. This flexibility is crucial for adapting to global economic trends and seizing opportunities in emerging sectors.

5. Innovation and Research Funding:
An independent Scotland can allocate resources to research and innovation based on its economic priorities. This includes investing in sectors such as technology, healthcare, and renewable energy, fostering economic growth and competitiveness.

6. Employment and Labor Policies:
Independence allows Scotland to develop labor policies tailored to its unique economic circumstances. This involves shaping employment

regulations, workers' rights, and training programs to address the specific needs of the Scottish workforce.

7. Financial Regulation:
Full control over financial regulations ensures that Scotland can establish a regulatory framework that meets the requirements of its financial institutions and economic ecosystem. This autonomy is vital for maintaining financial stability and confidence.

8. Infrastructure Investment:
Independence provides the ability to prioritize and direct infrastructure investments to address the specific needs of Scotland's regions. This includes transportation, communication, and energy

infrastructure that supports economic development.

9. Currency Policy:
The option of an independent currency allows Scotland to tailor its monetary policy to suit its economic conditions. This flexibility provides an additional tool for managing inflation, interest rates, and overall economic stability.

10. Economic Resilience and Crisis Response:
An independent Scotland can build economic resilience by designing policies that address vulnerabilities and enhance adaptability. Moreover, it can respond more efficiently to economic crises by implementing targeted measures that align with the nation's unique economic challenges.

In conclusion, the pursuit of economic control through independence is a central theme in the discourse on Scottish self-governance. Proponents argue that by gaining control over economic policies and resources, Scotland can position itself to address challenges, seize opportunities, and build a more prosperous and resilient economic future.

4

Resource Management and Economic Advantage: The Case for Independent Control Over Natural Resources in Scotland

One of the compelling arguments in favor of Scottish independence revolves around the notion of direct control over natural resources, particularly oil. Advocates argue that this autonomy over resource management can be a significant benefit, offering Scotland a unique economic advantage and the ability to shape its economic destiny.

1. Strategic Resource Utilization: Independence empowers Scotland to strategically utilize its natural resources, particularly North Sea oil. Direct control allows for a nuanced approach to extraction, production, and distribution, ensuring long-term sustainability and maximizing economic benefits.

2. Economic Stabilization: Control over oil resources provides an avenue for economic stabilization. During periods of global economic uncertainty, an independent Scotland can leverage its oil reserves to offset economic challenges, bolstering fiscal stability and ensuring continued public services.

3. Revenue Generation:
Direct control over oil resources enables Scotland to directly benefit from the revenue generated. The nation can determine taxation and royalty rates, ensuring that the economic returns from resource extraction contribute to national development and public welfare.

4. Diversification Opportunities:
With independent control, Scotland can explore opportunities for diversifying its energy portfolio. This includes investing in renewable energy sources, aligning with global trends towards sustainability and positioning

Scotland as a leader in green technologies.

5. Tailored Economic Policies:
Resource management independence facilitates the crafting of economic policies that align specifically with Scotland's economic goals. This includes investment in infrastructure, technology, and social programs, all shaped by the revenue streams from natural resources.

6. Job Creation and Skill Development:
Direct control over natural resources allows for the creation of employment opportunities and skill development initiatives. By strategically managing resource extraction, Scotland can stimulate job growth and ensure that its

workforce is equipped for the evolving demands of the energy sector.

7. Environmental Sustainability:
Independence provides the platform to implement environmental policies aligned with Scotland's unique landscapes. This includes stringent regulations to ensure responsible resource extraction, minimizing ecological impact and prioritizing long-term sustainability.

8. Negotiation Strength in Global Markets:
As an independent entity, Scotland can negotiate trade agreements and partnerships based on its own terms, leveraging its natural resources as strategic assets. This negotiation strength can lead to favorable

economic relationships on the global stage.

9. Innovation and Research Investment:
Control over natural resources allows for targeted investment in research and innovation. Scotland can fund initiatives that explore cutting-edge technologies and practices within the energy sector, fostering innovation and maintaining competitiveness.

10. Regional Development:
Independence facilitates regional development strategies that ensure communities near resource-rich areas directly benefit from resource extraction. This approach can contribute to balanced economic growth and address regional disparities.

In conclusion, proponents of Scottish independence argue that direct control over natural resources, particularly oil, provides a unique opportunity for economic self-determination. They contend that by managing these resources independently, Scotland can not only secure economic advantages but also contribute to sustainable development and long-term prosperity.

5

Tailored Policies for Scottish Prosperity: The Potential Benefits of Independence

A key argument in support of Scottish independence centers around the idea that self-governance provides the opportunity to craft policies that are finely tuned to meet the unique needs and aspirations of the Scottish people. This flexibility is seen as a means to foster sustainable development, address specific challenges, and build a resilient and prosperous future.

1. Cultural Preservation and Promotion:
Independence allows for the creation of policies that actively preserve and promote Scottish culture. This includes support for linguistic diversity, cultural heritage initiatives, and the elevation of Scottish arts, reinforcing a sense of identity and pride.

2. Social Welfare Tailoring:
An independent Scotland can design social welfare policies that directly respond to the social and economic challenges specific to its population.

Tailored initiatives may address issues such as poverty, education access, and healthcare in ways that reflect Scottish values and priorities.

3. Economic Diversification Strategies:
Independence provides the flexibility to implement economic diversification strategies. Scotland can design policies that encourage the growth of emerging industries, reducing dependence on specific sectors and enhancing overall economic resilience.

4. Regional Development Initiatives:
Tailored policies enable a focus on regional development, addressing the unique needs of different parts of Scotland. This approach can foster balanced economic growth, ensuring

that the benefits of development are spread across urban and rural areas.

5. Education System Alignment:
An independent Scotland can shape its education policies to align with its economic and cultural goals. This includes curriculum adjustments, emphasis on vocational training, and fostering innovation in educational practices to meet the needs of a rapidly evolving job market.

6. Healthcare Solutions for Scottish Well-being:
Independence allows for the design of healthcare policies that cater to the specific health challenges and priorities of the Scottish population. Tailoring healthcare strategies ensures efficient and targeted responses to public health issues.

7. Environmental Sustainability Initiatives:
Scotland can implement environmental policies that align with its unique natural landscapes. Tailored strategies for sustainable development, conservation efforts, and renewable energy adoption can be crafted to harmonize with the country's ecological diversity.

8. Agriculture and Rural Support:
Tailored policies can address the distinctive challenges faced by Scotland's agricultural and rural communities. Independence provides the opportunity to create agricultural subsidies, land-use policies, and rural development initiatives that suit the specific needs of Scottish farmers and residents.

9. Innovation and Technology Advancements:
Independence allows Scotland to foster innovation and technological advancements through policies that incentivize research and development. Tailored strategies can position Scotland at the forefront of emerging technologies, contributing to economic growth.

10. Social Inclusion and Equality:
An independent Scotland can actively pursue policies that promote social inclusion and equality. By tailoring initiatives to address specific social disparities, the nation can work towards building a more just and equitable society.

In summary, the argument for tailored policies under Scottish independence revolves around the idea that self-governance provides the freedom to respond to unique challenges and opportunities. Advocates believe that this flexibility allows Scotland to shape its own destiny in a way that best serves the well-being and aspirations of its citizens.

6

Social Policies for Scottish Well-Being: The Case for Independent Decision-Making

The pursuit of Scottish independence is strongly linked to the desire for self-determination, particularly in shaping social policies that address the specific needs and values of the Scottish people. The argument in favor of independence emphasizes the potential benefits of autonomously crafting social policies tailored to the distinctive socio-cultural landscape of Scotland.

1. Healthcare Prioritization: Independence grants Scotland the ability to prioritize and structure its healthcare policies based on the unique health challenges and priorities of its population. This includes decisions on funding allocations, healthcare infrastructure, and public health campaigns.

2. Education System Tailoring: An independent Scotland can shape its education policies to meet the specific demands of its society. This involves decisions on curriculum design, educational resources, and the emphasis on subjects that align with Scottish cultural, historical, and economic priorities.

3. Social Welfare Customization: The ability to independently design social welfare policies allows Scotland to address poverty, unemployment, and social inequality in ways that resonate with its values. Tailored initiatives can provide targeted support to vulnerable populations.

4. Family and Gender Equality: Independence provides the freedom to implement policies that foster gender equality and support families. Scotland can shape parental leave policies, childcare support, and initiatives to promote work-life balance in line with its societal aspirations.

5. Housing and Urban Development Strategies:
Autonomy in social policies allows for the customization of strategies addressing housing and urban development. Scotland can design initiatives that tackle issues such as affordable housing, homelessness, and sustainable urban planning based on its unique context.

6. Social Inclusion and Diversity:
Independence enables Scotland to proactively address issues of social inclusion and cultural diversity. Tailored policies can promote inclusivity, celebrate cultural diversity, and foster a sense of belonging among all residents.

7. Criminal Justice and Legal Reforms:
An independent Scotland can reform its criminal justice system and legal frameworks to align with its societal values. This includes decisions on policing, sentencing, and rehabilitation strategies tailored to the needs and expectations of Scottish communities.

8. Mental Health and Well-being Initiatives:
Tailoring mental health policies to the specific needs of the Scottish population becomes feasible with independence. Scotland can implement strategies that address mental health stigma, increase accessibility to mental health services, and prioritize well-being.

9. Social Care and Elderly Support:
Independence allows for the development of social care policies that cater to the aging population. Scotland can design initiatives to support the elderly, ensuring dignity, quality of life, and accessibility to necessary services.

10. Community Engagement and Participation:
Autonomous decision-making enables Scotland to design policies that encourage community engagement and participation. This involves strategies to empower local communities, enhance civic participation, and strengthen social bonds.

In summary, the ability to shape social policies independently of the rest of the

UK is considered a cornerstone of the argument for Scottish independence. Advocates contend that this autonomy provides the opportunity to create a society that reflects the values, priorities, and unique characteristics of the Scottish people.

7

Representation for Scotland: The Case for Independent Governance and Direct Advocacy

A central theme in the discourse surrounding Scottish independence is the idea that self-governance provides a pathway to more direct representation of Scottish interests. Advocates argue that by becoming an independent entity, Scotland can shape its political landscape in a way that better reflects the aspirations and priorities of its citizens.

1. Political Autonomy:
Independence allows Scotland to establish its own political institutions and decision-making processes. This autonomy ensures that political representation is directly aligned with the will of the Scottish electorate, free from the constraints of a larger political union.

2. Policy Alignment with Scottish Priorities:
An independent Scotland can tailor policies to specifically address the priorities and challenges faced by its population. Direct representation ensures that the government is responsive to the unique economic, social, and cultural needs of Scotland.

3. Effective Advocacy in International Forums:
As an independent nation, Scotland gains the ability to represent its interests directly in international forums. This includes participation in organizations such as the United Nations, where Scotland can advocate for issues important to its citizens on the global stage.

4. Tailored Foreign Policy:
Independence provides the freedom to shape foreign policy that aligns with Scottish values and interests. Scotland can establish diplomatic relationships and engage in international affairs based on its unique geopolitical position and priorities.

5. Protection of Scottish Institutions:
Direct representation allows for the protection and enhancement of Scottish institutions. Scotland can design its own governance structures, ensuring that they reflect the cultural and historical uniqueness of the nation.

6. Economic Decision-Making:
With independence, Scotland can make economic decisions that directly benefit its citizens. This includes choices related to taxation, public spending, and economic development, all aligned with the specific economic goals of Scotland.

7. Cultural Identity Promotion:
Direct representation enables Scotland to actively promote and protect its cultural identity. Policies can be

crafted to support linguistic diversity, cultural heritage, and artistic endeavors, fostering a sense of pride and continuity.

8. Regional Representation:
Independence facilitates a more granular approach to regional representation. Scotland can ensure that the diverse regions within the country have a direct voice in shaping policies that impact their specific needs and challenges.

9. Responsive Governance:
A government directly accountable to the Scottish people is inherently more responsive. Independent governance allows for agile decision-making and the ability to swiftly address emerging issues or changing circumstances.

10. Democratic Legitimacy:
Direct representation enhances the democratic legitimacy of the Scottish government. Policies and decisions are made by elected representatives accountable to the Scottish electorate, strengthening the connection between the government and the governed.

In summary, the pursuit of Scottish independence is often framed as a quest for more direct representation of Scottish interests. Proponents argue that by establishing independent governance, Scotland can tailor its political and policy landscape to better serve the diverse needs and aspirations of its citizens.

International Relations: Scotland's Path to Diplomatic Independence

A pivotal aspect of the argument for Scottish independence is the opportunity to establish and manage its own diplomatic relationships on the global stage. Advocates contend that this autonomy in international relations allows Scotland to shape its foreign policy, engage in diplomatic initiatives, and represent its interests more directly in the international community.

1. Sovereign Diplomacy: Independence provides Scotland with the status of a sovereign nation, allowing it to conduct its own diplomatic affairs. This independence is fundamental to shaping foreign policy that aligns precisely with Scottish interests, unhindered by the considerations of a larger political union.

2. Tailored Foreign Policy Priorities:
As an independent entity, Scotland can craft foreign policy priorities that reflect its unique economic, political, and cultural circumstances. This includes decisions on trade, security, climate change, and humanitarian efforts based on Scotland's specific values and goals.

3. Representation in International Organizations:
Independence affords Scotland the opportunity to secure direct representation in international organizations. This includes participation in forums such as the United Nations, where Scotland can

advocate for global issues that align with its values and priorities.

4. Economic Diplomacy:
Scotland can engage in economic diplomacy tailored to its economic goals. Independent diplomatic initiatives can focus on attracting foreign investment, negotiating trade agreements, and promoting Scottish industries and exports.

5. Cultural Diplomacy:
An independent Scotland can actively engage in cultural diplomacy to promote its unique heritage and identity. This involves initiatives such as cultural exchanges, arts promotion, and collaboration with international partners to raise awareness of Scottish culture.

6. Human Rights Advocacy:
Independence provides the platform for Scotland to independently advocate for human rights on the global stage. The nation can contribute to international efforts to address human rights abuses and promote social justice based on its own principles and values.

7. Conflict Resolution and Peacekeeping:
As an independent actor, Scotland can contribute to conflict resolution and peacekeeping efforts in a manner consistent with its values. This may involve participation in international peacekeeping missions or diplomatic interventions in global conflicts.

8. Climate Change Collaboration:
Scotland, with independence, can actively engage in international efforts

to combat climate change. The nation can negotiate climate agreements, share best practices, and contribute to global initiatives aimed at environmental sustainability.

9. Health and Pandemic Response Cooperation:
Independence enables Scotland to establish its own diplomatic relationships for international health cooperation. This includes collaboration on pandemic response, healthcare initiatives, and contributions to global health organizations.

10. Global Partnerships Based on Scottish Interests:
An independent Scotland can build strategic partnerships with countries and organizations that align with its interests. These partnerships can

extend beyond historical ties, allowing Scotland to forge relationships based on contemporary economic, political, and cultural affinities.

In summary, the ability to establish its own diplomatic relationships is a crucial aspect of the argument for Scottish independence. Proponents emphasize that this diplomatic autonomy enables Scotland to navigate the complexities of the international arena with a direct focus on its unique values, interests, and priorities.

9

European Union Access: The Potential Implications of Scottish Independence

A significant facet of the debate around Scottish independence is the question of European Union (EU) access. Proponents of independence argue that it could afford Scotland the opportunity to rejoin or maintain closer ties with the EU. Here are some considerations in favor of this perspective:

1. Sovereign Decision-Making: Independence would empower Scotland to make its own decisions regarding EU membership. This sovereign decision-making process allows Scotland to negotiate its relationship with the EU based on its unique circumstances and preferences.

2. Economic Benefits of EU Membership:

Rejoining the EU or establishing closer ties could provide economic benefits for Scotland. Access to the EU single market and participation in its economic policies may contribute to trade advantages, investment opportunities, and economic stability.

3. Free Movement of People:
EU membership or a close relationship with the EU could facilitate the continuation of the free movement of people. This is particularly relevant for issues such as labor mobility, education exchanges, and cultural interactions, which align with the principles of the EU.

4. Research and Innovation Opportunities:
Closer ties with the EU could enhance Scotland's participation in EU-funded

research and innovation programs. This collaboration may contribute to advancements in science, technology, and various industries, fostering innovation and economic growth.

5. Social and Environmental Standards:
Adopting or aligning with EU standards on social issues and environmental regulations might be an attractive prospect for an independent Scotland. This alignment could demonstrate a commitment to shared values regarding workers' rights, environmental protection, and social justice.

6. International Collaboration and Influence:
EU membership or strong ties could bolster Scotland's influence on the

international stage. Participation in EU decision-making processes and collaborative efforts amplifies Scotland's voice in global affairs, potentially enhancing diplomatic and geopolitical significance.

7. Regional Cohesion and Solidarity:
EU membership promotes regional cohesion and solidarity. An independent Scotland's inclusion in the EU could strengthen ties with neighboring countries, fostering cooperation on shared challenges, and promoting regional stability.

8. Access to EU Programs:
Rejoining the EU or maintaining close ties could provide Scotland access to various EU programs and initiatives. These cover a broad spectrum,

including educational programs, cultural exchanges, and initiatives supporting social and economic development.

9. Legal and Regulatory Framework:
Alignment with EU legal and regulatory frameworks may offer stability and consistency for businesses and citizens in an independent Scotland. This alignment could simplify legal processes and regulatory compliance, contributing to economic efficiency.

10. Mitigating Brexit Consequences:
For those who favored remaining in the EU during the Brexit referendum, Scottish independence offers a potential means to mitigate the

consequences of Brexit. Rejoining the EU or establishing close ties might be perceived as a way to maintain certain benefits associated with EU membership.

In conclusion, the prospect of EU access is a significant element in the discussions surrounding Scottish independence. Advocates argue that such access could bring economic advantages, strengthen international ties, and allow Scotland to participate in a collaborative, multinational community with shared values and interests.

10

Defense Policies for Scottish Interests: The Case for Independence

One key argument in favor of Scottish independence revolves around the idea that an independent Scotland would have the ability to determine defense strategies tailored to its specific interests and needs. Advocates argue that this autonomy in defense policy would allow Scotland to address its unique security challenges and align military capabilities with its priorities.

1. Regional Security Focus: Independence would empower Scotland to tailor its defense policies to address regional security challenges specific to its geographic location. This may involve prioritizing maritime security, cyber threats, or cooperation with neighboring countries on shared security concerns.

2. Armed Forces Structure:
An independent Scotland could reshape its armed forces structure to align with its specific defense requirements. This might involve optimizing the size, capabilities, and focus areas of the military to efficiently address identified threats and vulnerabilities.

3. Non-Nuclear Stance:
Scotland's stance on nuclear weapons has been a significant point of discussion. Independence would allow Scotland to pursue a non-nuclear policy if desired, determining its approach to disarmament or adopting alternative defense strategies that align with its commitment to a nuclear-free stance.

4. Multinational Defense Collaboration:
Independence could enable Scotland to engage in defense collaboration with other nations on its own terms. The nation could selectively participate in multinational defense efforts, fostering partnerships based on shared interests and goals rather than obligations from a larger political union.

5. Cybersecurity Focus:
As an independent entity, Scotland could prioritize and invest in cybersecurity capabilities to protect against emerging threats in the digital domain. Tailoring defense strategies to address cyber vulnerabilities would be critical in securing national interests.

6. Humanitarian and Peacekeeping Initiatives:

An independent Scotland could shape its defense policies to align with a commitment to humanitarian and peacekeeping efforts. Participation in international peacekeeping missions and the provision of humanitarian aid may reflect the nation's values and priorities.

7. Intelligence and Counterterrorism Measures:
Independence would provide the flexibility to enhance intelligence capabilities and counterterrorism measures. Scotland could develop specialized units and collaborate with international partners to address specific threats to its security.

8. Border Security and Immigration Control:

Tailoring defense policies would allow Scotland to address challenges related to border security and immigration control based on its unique circumstances. This might involve cooperation with neighboring countries or the development of specific border security measures.

9. Resilience and Disaster Response:
Independence could lead to the development of defense policies that focus on enhancing resilience and disaster response capabilities. Scotland could prepare for and respond to natural disasters or other emergencies, safeguarding the well-being of its citizens.

10. Budget Allocation and Resource Management:

An independent Scotland would have control over defense budget allocation and resource management. This autonomy would allow the nation to invest in defense capabilities that directly align with its identified security priorities, ensuring an efficient and effective use of resources.

In summary, the ability to determine defense strategies based on specific Scottish interests is a core argument in favor of independence. Advocates contend that this autonomy would enable Scotland to adopt a defense posture that best serves its unique security challenges and aligns with the nation's values and aspirations.

11

Healthcare Policies: Tailoring Strategies for Scottish Well-being through Independence

A compelling argument in favor of Scottish independence is the potential to shape healthcare policies that are finely tuned to address the specific health challenges and priorities of the Scottish population. Proponents contend that an independent Scotland could design and implement strategies tailored to the nation's unique context, fostering a healthier and more resilient society.

1. Public Health Prioritization: Independence provides the opportunity to prioritize public health initiatives based on the specific health challenges faced by Scotland. Tailored policies can address prevalent issues such as cardiovascular disease, mental health, and public health crises.

2. Chronic Disease Management:
Tailoring healthcare policies enables a focused approach to chronic disease management. An independent Scotland could develop targeted interventions and support systems to address prevalent chronic conditions, improving overall health outcomes.

3. Rural and Urban Health Disparities:
Independence allows for a nuanced response to the health disparities between rural and urban areas. Tailored policies can address the unique challenges faced by each region, ensuring that healthcare resources are distributed equitably.

4. Health Workforce Planning:
An independent Scotland could design healthcare workforce strategies that meet the specific needs of its population. This includes training programs, recruitment initiatives, and policies to address shortages in critical healthcare professions.

5. Mental Health Support:
Tailored healthcare policies can prioritize mental health support, addressing the unique mental health challenges faced by the Scottish population. Initiatives may focus on prevention, early intervention, and destigmatization of mental health issues.

6. Substance Abuse Prevention and Treatment:

Independence allows for a comprehensive approach to substance abuse prevention and treatment. Tailored policies can include education programs, harm reduction strategies, and specialized services to combat substance abuse challenges.

7. Integration of Social Care:
An independent Scotland can integrate social care seamlessly into healthcare policies. This holistic approach ensures that healthcare strategies consider social determinants of health, promoting overall well-being and reducing health inequalities.

8. Health Innovation and Research:
Tailored policies can foster innovation in healthcare research and technology. Independence provides the opportunity

to invest in cutting-edge medical research, develop innovative treatments, and enhance healthcare delivery methods.

9. Community-Based Healthcare:
Independence allows for the development of community-based healthcare models. Tailored policies can encourage the establishment of local healthcare services that cater to the specific needs and preferences of diverse communities.

10. Pandemic Preparedness and Response:
An independent Scotland could tailor healthcare policies to enhance pandemic preparedness and response. This includes robust surveillance systems, efficient distribution of medical resources, and the

development of a resilient healthcare infrastructure.

11. Data Privacy and Healthcare Information Management: Independence enables the establishment of tailored policies regarding data privacy and healthcare information management. Scotland can design secure and ethical systems to manage healthcare data, ensuring patient confidentiality and supporting medical research.

In conclusion, the argument for independence often includes the potential to shape healthcare policies that directly respond to the unique health challenges of the Scottish population. Advocates argue that this autonomy in healthcare decision-making can lead to a more responsive, equitable, and effective healthcare system for the benefit of all Scots.

12

Education System Autonomy: Nurturing a Distinctive Path for Scotland's Future

A central argument in favor of Scottish independence is the prospect of having autonomy in shaping education policies. Proponents contend that this independence allows Scotland to design an education system finely tuned to meet its unique needs, foster cultural identity, and equip its citizens with the skills needed for a dynamic and globally competitive future.

1. Curriculum Design and Flexibility:

Independence provides the opportunity to design a curriculum that aligns with Scotland's cultural, historical, and economic priorities. A tailored curriculum can reflect the nation's values and aspirations, ensuring that students receive an education that is relevant and meaningful to their lives.

2. Emphasis on Scottish History and Culture:
An autonomous education system allows Scotland to place a stronger emphasis on its own history, literature, and cultural heritage. This can instill a sense of pride and identity among students, fostering a deep connection to the nation's rich traditions.

3. Language Policies and Linguistic Diversity:

Independence enables Scotland to set language policies that support and preserve linguistic diversity. The education system can actively promote the use of Scots and Scottish Gaelic, preserving these languages as integral components of Scottish identity.

4. Tailored Approaches to Teaching and Learning:
Autonomy in education policies allows for innovative approaches to teaching and learning. Scotland can explore pedagogical methods that cater to the diverse learning styles and needs of its students, fostering a dynamic and engaging educational experience.

5. Vocational Education and Skills Training:
An independent Scotland can prioritize vocational education and skills training

based on its economic goals. The education system can be designed to equip students with the practical skills needed for success in specific industries, contributing to economic growth and job creation.

6. Inclusive Education and Diversity:
Autonomous education policies can promote inclusivity and diversity within the curriculum. Scotland can design strategies to ensure that the education system reflects and celebrates the diverse backgrounds, cultures, and perspectives of its student population.

7. Higher Education Funding and Access:
Independence allows for control over higher education funding and access.

Scotland can design policies to ensure affordable and accessible higher education, supporting the aspirations of its citizens and fostering a well-educated and skilled workforce.

8. Research and Innovation Investment:
An independent Scotland can strategically invest in research and innovation within its education system. This includes fostering collaboration between universities, research institutions, and industries to drive advancements in science, technology, and other fields.

9. Teacher Training and Professional Development:
Autonomy enables Scotland to shape teacher training and professional development programs that align with

its educational goals. This includes ensuring that educators are equipped with the skills and knowledge necessary to deliver high-quality education.

10. Educational Infrastructure Investment:
Independence provides the platform to prioritize and invest in educational infrastructure. Scotland can direct resources to modernize schools, improve technology in classrooms, and create a conducive learning environment that meets the evolving needs of students.

In conclusion, autonomy in education policies is seen as a key advantage of Scottish independence, offering the opportunity to craft an education system that reflects the nation's values, preserves its cultural heritage, and equips its citizens for success in an ever-changing world. Advocates argue that this independence in education is foundational to shaping a brighter and more prosperous future for Scotland.

13

Environmental Policies: Shaping a Sustainable Future through Independence

A compelling argument in favor of Scottish independence centers around the ability to exercise independent control over environmental policies. Proponents assert that this autonomy allows Scotland to tailor regulations and sustainability initiatives to its specific ecological landscape, fostering environmental stewardship and addressing global challenges.

1. Tailored Environmental Regulations:
Independence provides Scotland with the flexibility to design environmental regulations that address its unique ecosystems and conservation needs. This includes setting standards for air and water quality, waste management, and biodiversity protection based on the nation's distinct environmental challenges.

2. Climate Change Mitigation Strategies:
An autonomous Scotland can implement targeted climate change mitigation strategies aligned with its specific geography and climate patterns. This may involve renewable

energy investments, emissions reduction targets, and initiatives to enhance climate resilience.

3. Conservation and Biodiversity Protection:
Independence allows Scotland to adopt conservation measures that preserve its diverse ecosystems and protect endangered species. The nation can design policies to safeguard natural habitats, prevent habitat loss, and promote biodiversity conservation.

4. Renewable Energy Development:
Scotland's independence enables the nation to strategically invest in renewable energy development. Policies can be crafted to support the expansion of wind, solar, hydro, and other renewable sources, positioning

Scotland as a leader in sustainable energy production.

5. Circular Economy Initiatives: Autonomy in environmental policies allows Scotland to champion circular economy initiatives. This involves minimizing waste, promoting recycling and reuse, and fostering sustainable production practices to reduce the environmental impact of consumption.

6. Marine and Coastal Protection: Independence enables Scotland to implement robust policies for the protection of its marine and coastal environments. This may include measures to combat plastic pollution, regulate fisheries sustainably, and preserve the health of coastal ecosystems.

7. Community Engagement in Environmental Conservation:
An autonomous Scotland can design policies that actively engage communities in environmental conservation efforts. This includes initiatives to raise awareness, encourage sustainable practices, and empower local communities to participate in environmental stewardship.

8. Sustainable Agriculture Practices:
Independence allows Scotland to set policies promoting sustainable agriculture practices. This may involve supporting organic farming, reducing reliance on harmful pesticides, and incentivizing practices that prioritize soil health and biodiversity.

9. Natural Resource Management:
Autonomous control over environmental policies extends to natural resource management. Scotland can adopt strategies for responsible extraction of resources, ensuring that economic activities align with long-term ecological sustainability.

10. International Environmental Collaboration:
Independence provides Scotland the opportunity to engage in international environmental collaborations on its own terms. The nation can contribute to global efforts on issues such as climate change, conservation, and sustainable development, leveraging its unique perspectives and strengths.

In summary, the argument for independent control over

environmental policies in Scotland emphasizes the potential to shape a sustainable future. Proponents assert that this autonomy allows the nation to address its environmental challenges strategically, contribute to global environmental goals, and serve as a model for responsible and sustainable governance.

14

Fiscal Policy Independence: Shaping Scotland's Economic Destiny

A pivotal argument in favor of Scottish independence revolves around the autonomy to set fiscal policies, including tax strategies and economic frameworks. Proponents contend that this independence empowers Scotland to craft economic policies tailored to its unique needs, driving sustainable growth and addressing specific challenges.

1. Taxation Autonomy:
Independence grants Scotland the ability to set its own tax policies. This includes decisions on income tax rates, corporate taxes, and other levies, allowing the nation to design a tax system that aligns with its economic goals and societal values.

2. Economic Diversification:
An independent Scotland can pursue economic diversification strategies tailored to its strengths and opportunities. Fiscal policies can incentivize the growth of emerging industries, reducing dependence on specific sectors and enhancing overall economic resilience.

3. Social Welfare Investment:
Fiscal policy independence enables Scotland to determine the allocation of resources for social welfare programs. The nation can design policies that prioritize healthcare, education, and social services, addressing societal needs in a way that reflects its values.

4. Infrastructure Investment:
Control over fiscal policies allows for strategic infrastructure investment. Scotland can direct resources to critical infrastructure projects, fostering economic development, enhancing connectivity, and creating jobs.

5. Innovation and Research Funding:
An independent Scotland can allocate funds to support innovation and

research. Fiscal policies can incentivize private and public investment in research and development, positioning Scotland at the forefront of technological advancements.

6. Responsive Economic Stimulus:
Independence enables Scotland to respond swiftly to economic challenges. Fiscal policies can be designed to include targeted economic stimulus measures during downturns, ensuring a nimble and effective response to changing economic conditions.

7. Regional Development Incentives:
Fiscal autonomy allows for the implementation of regional

development incentives. Scotland can craft policies that encourage economic growth in specific regions, addressing disparities and promoting balanced development across the nation.

8. Debt Management Strategies:
An independent Scotland can develop its own strategies for managing public debt. Fiscal policies can prioritize responsible debt management while ensuring the necessary investments for economic growth and stability.

9. Job Creation Initiatives:
Fiscal policies can be tailored to incentivize job creation. Scotland can design strategies to support small and medium-sized enterprises (SMEs), stimulate entrepreneurship, and foster an environment conducive to sustainable employment opportunities.

10. Economic Resilience Planning:
Independence provides the autonomy to develop economic resilience plans. Fiscal policies can include contingency measures, risk management strategies, and long-term economic planning to navigate global uncertainties and challenges.

In summary, the argument for fiscal policy independence underpins the case for Scottish independence. Proponents assert that the ability to set tax policies and economic strategies independently allows Scotland to take charge of its economic destiny, fostering sustainable growth, addressing societal needs, and responding effectively to the dynamic global economic landscape.

15

Social Welfare Autonomy: Crafting Programs Aligned with Scottish Priorities

A central tenet of the argument for Scottish independence is the prospect of having autonomy in designing social welfare programs that closely align with the unique priorities of the Scottish population. Proponents emphasize that this independence allows for the tailoring of social policies to address specific needs, fostering a fair and inclusive society.

1. Targeted Poverty Alleviation: Independence provides the opportunity to design social welfare programs that effectively target and alleviate poverty in Scotland. Tailored policies can address the root causes of poverty, ensuring that support reaches those who need it most.

2. Affordable Housing Initiatives: An independent Scotland can shape social welfare policies to tackle the challenges of affordable housing. This may include strategies to increase housing availability, rent controls, and incentives for sustainable and affordable housing development.

3. Accessible Healthcare for All: Autonomy allows for the design of healthcare policies that prioritize accessibility for all citizens. Scotland can develop initiatives to ensure affordable healthcare services, reduce health inequalities, and promote overall well-being.

4. Childcare Support and Family Benefits:
Independence enables the customization of childcare support and family benefits. Social welfare programs can be crafted to provide financial assistance to families, ensuring the well-being and development of children.

5. Education Equality and Access:
An independent Scotland can design social welfare policies to promote education equality and access. Initiatives may include financial support for students, programs to address educational disparities, and measures to enhance access to quality education for all.

6. Social Inclusion for Vulnerable Groups:
Autonomy allows for the development of social welfare programs that actively promote social inclusion for vulnerable groups. This includes support for individuals with disabilities, refugees, and other marginalized communities.

7. Unemployment Support and Job Training:
Independence provides the flexibility to design unemployment support and job training programs tailored to the needs of the Scottish workforce. Social welfare initiatives can focus on equipping individuals with the skills needed for sustainable employment.

8. Elderly Care and Support:

An independent Scotland can address the specific needs of its aging population through tailored social welfare programs. This may involve initiatives to support elderly care, enhance social inclusion for seniors, and provide financial assistance.

9. Mental Health and Well-being Services:
Autonomy in social welfare allows for a dedicated focus on mental health and well-being services. Scotland can design programs to destigmatize mental health issues, increase access to mental health services, and promote overall psychological well-being.

10. Community Empowerment Initiatives:
Independence enables the development of social welfare programs that

empower local communities. Initiatives may include community-led projects, funding for grassroots organizations, and strategies to enhance civic engagement and participation.

In summary, the argument for social welfare autonomy within the context of Scottish independence emphasizes the capacity to design programs that reflect the values and priorities of the Scottish people. Proponents contend that this independence allows for a more responsive, inclusive, and compassionate approach to social policies, contributing to the well-being of the entire Scottish population.

Innovation and Technology Autonomy: Fostering Scotland's Future Prosperity

A compelling argument in favor of Scottish independence centers around the autonomy to tailor policies that specifically foster innovation and technological advancements. Proponents contend that this independence empowers Scotland to create an environment conducive to research, development, and technological progress, driving economic growth and global competitiveness.

1. Research and Development Investment:
Independence allows Scotland to strategically invest in research and development (R&D). Tailored policies

can prioritize funding for innovation across various sectors, fostering a culture of discovery and advancement.

2. Technology Incubators and Start-Up Support:
An autonomous Scotland can establish technology incubators and support systems for start-ups. Policies can be designed to encourage entrepreneurship, providing resources, mentorship, and funding to foster the growth of innovative tech companies.

3. Educational Focus on STEM:
Independence enables the customization of educational policies to emphasize science, technology, engineering, and mathematics (STEM) disciplines. A tailored educational approach can prepare the workforce

with the skills needed for a technology-driven future.

4. Collaboration between Industry and Academia:
Autonomy allows for the facilitation of collaboration between industry and academia. Policies can encourage partnerships that promote the transfer of knowledge, expertise, and resources, accelerating technological innovation.

5. Incentives for Tech Companies and Research Institutions:
Independence provides the flexibility to design incentives for technology companies and research institutions. Policies can include tax breaks, grants, and other benefits to encourage investment in innovation, attracting both domestic and international players.

6. Digital Infrastructure Investment:
An independent Scotland can prioritize investment in digital infrastructure. Policies can focus on building robust and high-speed connectivity, ensuring that the nation is at the forefront of the digital revolution.

7. Regulation for Emerging Technologies:
Autonomy allows for the creation of responsive regulations for emerging technologies. Policies can be crafted to ensure ethical and responsible development, while providing a regulatory environment that supports innovation in areas like artificial intelligence and biotechnology.

8. Cybersecurity Strategies:

Independence enables the development of robust cybersecurity strategies. Policies can be tailored to address the evolving threats in the digital landscape, ensuring the protection of critical infrastructure and fostering a secure environment for innovation.

9. Smart City Initiatives:
An autonomous Scotland can implement smart city initiatives. Policies can encourage the adoption of technology to enhance urban living, improve sustainability, and create efficient, interconnected urban environments.

10. Green Technology and Sustainability:
Independence provides the platform to prioritize green technology and sustainability. Policies can incentivize

the development and adoption of environmentally friendly technologies, positioning Scotland as a leader in sustainable innovation.

11. Global Technology Partnerships:
Autonomy allows for the establishment of global technology partnerships. Scotland can actively engage in collaborations with other nations and international tech organizations, fostering a dynamic exchange of ideas and expertise.

In summary, the argument for innovation and technology autonomy within the context of Scottish independence emphasizes the potential to create a dynamic and forward-looking society. Proponents contend that this independence allows Scotland

to harness the power of innovation,
driving economic growth, fostering job
creation, and positioning the nation as
a global leader in technological
advancement.

17

**Energy Transition Autonomy: A
Tailored Approach to Renewable
Energy in an Independent Scotland**

A key argument in favor of Scottish
independence is the potential for a
more tailored and focused approach to
transitioning to renewable energy
sources. Proponents assert that
independence provides the flexibility
to design policies that align
specifically with Scotland's unique
energy landscape, fostering

sustainability, and driving the transition towards a greener future.

1. Harnessing Renewable Resources:
Independence allows Scotland to leverage its abundant renewable resources, including wind, hydro, and tidal energy. Tailored policies can facilitate the development of projects that harness these resources, maximizing the nation's potential for clean energy production.

2. Offshore Wind Innovation:
An autonomous Scotland can lead innovation in offshore wind technology. Policies can be designed to support research, development, and implementation of cutting-edge technologies, positioning Scotland as a global leader in offshore wind energy.

3. Community-Led Renewable Projects:
Independence provides the opportunity for community-led renewable energy initiatives. Policies can encourage local communities to actively participate in and benefit from renewable projects, fostering a sense of ownership and shared responsibility for sustainable energy development.

4. Grid Modernization and Interconnectivity:
An independent Scotland can prioritize the modernization of its energy grid. Policies can support the development of a resilient and interconnected grid infrastructure, ensuring efficient distribution of renewable energy across the nation.

5. Incentives for Green Innovation:
Autonomy allows for the creation of incentives that spur green innovation. Policies can include tax breaks, grants, and subsidies to encourage businesses and individuals to invest in and adopt sustainable and energy-efficient technologies.

6. Renewable Heat Initiatives:
Independence enables the customization of policies to promote renewable heat initiatives. Strategies can focus on transitioning away from fossil fuels in heating systems, encouraging the adoption of renewable technologies such as heat pumps and solar thermal.

7. Energy Storage Solutions:

An autonomous Scotland can actively pursue energy storage solutions. Policies can support the development of advanced energy storage technologies, addressing the intermittency of renewable sources and enhancing the reliability of the energy grid.

8. Sustainable Transport Policies: Independence allows for the design of sustainable transport policies. Policies can incentivize the adoption of electric vehicles, invest in charging infrastructure, and promote sustainable modes of transportation, contributing to a reduction in carbon emissions.

9. Green Hydrogen Production: Autonomy provides the opportunity to lead in green hydrogen production. Policies can support research and development in this emerging sector, positioning Scotland as a key player in the production of hydrogen using renewable energy sources.

10. Circular Economy for Energy:
An independent Scotland can adopt a circular economy approach to energy. Policies can encourage recycling and repurposing of components in the renewable energy sector, minimizing waste and maximizing the sustainability of the entire energy lifecycle.

11. International Collaboration for Green Energy:
Independence enables Scotland to engage in international collaboration for green energy initiatives. The nation can pursue partnerships with other countries, share best practices, and

contribute to global efforts to combat climate change.

In conclusion, the argument for energy transition autonomy within the context of Scottish independence emphasizes the potential to lead a focused and impactful shift towards renewable energy. Proponents assert that this independence allows Scotland to develop a sustainable energy strategy that aligns with its unique strengths, contributing to environmental conservation and positioning the nation as a pioneer in the global transition to a greener future.

18

Legal System Autonomy: Shaping a Legal Framework Aligned with Scottish Values

A fundamental aspect of the argument for Scottish independence is the opportunity to have autonomy in shaping and adapting the legal system to reflect Scottish values, priorities, and preferences. Proponents contend that this independence in legal matters enables the creation of a legal framework that is more responsive to the specific needs of the Scottish people.

1. Legal Tradition and Cultural Identity:
Independence provides the opportunity to reinforce and preserve Scotland's distinct legal tradition. Tailoring the legal system allows for the incorporation and recognition of cultural values, linguistic nuances, and

historical context that are integral to Scottish identity.

2. Customized Legislation:
An autonomous Scotland can design legislation that is tailored to its unique circumstances. This includes the ability to create laws that specifically address social, economic, and environmental challenges faced by the nation, ensuring relevance and effectiveness.

3. Constitutional Autonomy:
Independence allows Scotland to define its own constitution. This provides the foundation for the legal system and allows for the establishment of the fundamental principles and rights that reflect the values and aspirations of the Scottish people.

4. Justice System Reforms:
Autonomy in legal matters permits the implementation of justice system reforms. Policies can be crafted to enhance access to justice, streamline legal processes, and ensure fairness and equity within the legal system.

5. Human Rights Protections:
An independent Scotland can reinforce its commitment to human rights through tailored legal protections. Policies can be designed to align with international human rights standards while considering specific Scottish values and priorities.

6. Environmental Legal Framework:
Independence enables the creation of an environmental legal framework that addresses Scotland's specific

environmental challenges. Policies can be developed to strengthen environmental protections, regulate resource use, and promote sustainability.

7. Social Justice Legislation:
Autonomy in legal matters allows for the development of social justice legislation. Policies can be crafted to address inequalities, protect vulnerable populations, and foster a more inclusive and equitable society.

8. Family Law and Cultural Considerations:
An independent Scotland can adapt family law to reflect cultural considerations. Policies can be designed to accommodate diverse family structures, inheritance

traditions, and marriage practices that are specific to Scottish culture.

9. Legal Language and Terminology:
Independence provides the opportunity to use legal language and terminology that resonates with the Scottish people. Policies can be drafted in a manner that is accessible and understandable to the general population, promoting legal literacy.

10. Judicial Appointments and Independence:
An autonomous Scotland can determine its own processes for judicial appointments, reinforcing the independence of the judiciary. This ensures that the legal system is equipped with judges who reflect the

values and diversity of Scottish society.

11. Alternative Dispute Resolution:
Independence allows for the promotion of alternative dispute resolution mechanisms. Policies can encourage mediation and arbitration as viable alternatives to traditional court proceedings, offering more flexible and efficient avenues for dispute resolution.

In summary, the argument for legal system autonomy within the context of Scottish independence emphasizes the capacity to shape a legal framework that is deeply rooted in Scottish values and adaptable to the nation's evolving needs. Proponents contend that this independence is foundational to fostering a legal system that is both reflective of and responsive to the unique characteristics and aspirations of the Scottish people.

19

Customs and Immigration Autonomy: Charting Scotland's Borders on Its Own Terms

A significant facet of the case for Scottish independence lies in the potential for autonomous control over customs and immigration policies. Proponents argue that this independence allows Scotland to tailor its approach to border control in a manner that aligns with its unique economic, social, and demographic considerations.

1. Tailored Immigration Policies:
Independence provides Scotland with the flexibility to design immigration policies that meet its specific needs. This includes setting criteria for skilled migration, family reunification, and addressing labor market demands in a manner that aligns with the nation's economic goals.

2. Regional Workforce Requirements:
An autonomous Scotland can address regional workforce requirements through tailored immigration policies. Policies can be designed to attract skilled workers to specific industries or regions where there may be a shortage of expertise.

3. Economic Contributions:

Independence allows Scotland to determine the criteria for immigrants based on their potential economic contributions. Policies can incentivize individuals with skills that are in high demand or those who are likely to make significant contributions to the economy.

4. Education and Research Collaboration:
Autonomy in immigration policies facilitates collaboration in education and research. Scotland can attract international students and researchers, fostering a dynamic academic environment and contributing to the nation's global standing in research and innovation.

5. Family Reunification Programs:

An independent Scotland can design family reunification programs that reflect its values and priorities. Policies can be crafted to facilitate the reunification of families, ensuring a compassionate and inclusive approach to immigration.

6. Humanitarian Considerations:
Independence provides the opportunity to address humanitarian considerations through immigration policies. Scotland can establish compassionate measures for refugees and asylum seekers, reflecting the nation's commitment to human rights and global solidarity.

7. Customs Control for Economic Efficiency:
Autonomy in customs policies allows for the streamlining of trade processes. Scotland can design customs controls

that prioritize economic efficiency, reducing trade barriers and ensuring the smooth flow of goods across its borders.

8. Trade Agreements and Negotiations:
An autonomous Scotland can engage in trade agreements and negotiations tailored to its economic interests. This includes the ability to negotiate trade deals that align with specific sectors, fostering economic growth and international collaboration.

9. Security and Border Protection:
Independence enables Scotland to customize security measures and border protection policies. The nation can develop strategies to address specific security challenges and ensure

the safety of its citizens while facilitating legitimate travel and trade.

10. Regional Collaboration:
Autonomy in customs and immigration policies allows for regional collaboration. Scotland can work closely with neighboring countries to develop coordinated approaches that enhance security, facilitate trade, and address shared challenges.

11. Public Opinion and Integration:
Independence provides the autonomy to consider public opinion and preferences in shaping immigration policies. This ensures that the policies are reflective of the values and sentiments of the Scottish population, promoting social cohesion and integration.

In conclusion, the argument for customs and immigration autonomy within the context of Scottish independence emphasizes the capacity to chart Scotland's borders based on its unique considerations. Proponents contend that this independence allows for a more responsive and tailored approach to immigration and customs policies, contributing to economic growth, social harmony, and national identity.

20

Direct Representation: Elevating Scotland's Voice on the Global Stage

A significant aspect of the case for Scottish independence is the opportunity for direct representation in international organizations, free from the constraints of the United Kingdom. Proponents argue that this autonomy enhances Scotland's ability to engage with the global community, allowing for more direct and impactful participation in international affairs.

1. Independent Diplomacy: Independence empowers Scotland to conduct its own independent diplomacy. This includes the ability to establish diplomatic missions, negotiate treaties, and engage directly with other nations, amplifying Scotland's presence and influence in global diplomatic circles.

2. Tailored Foreign Policy: An autonomous Scotland can craft foreign policies that align with its unique priorities and values. This flexibility allows Scotland to respond to international challenges in a way that reflects the aspirations and concerns of its citizens.

3. Direct Participation in Global Governance:
Independence provides Scotland with the opportunity for direct participation in global governance structures. This includes involvement in international organizations, such as the United Nations, where Scotland can contribute directly to discussions and decisions that impact global peace, security, and development.

4. Climate Change Advocacy:
Scotland, as an independent entity, can advocate for its own climate change policies on the international stage. This

includes participating directly in global climate negotiations, setting ambitious targets, and collaborating with other nations to address the urgent challenges posed by climate change.

5. Economic Representation: Autonomy allows Scotland to represent its economic interests directly in international forums. This includes participating in trade negotiations, advocating for market access, and promoting Scotland's industries on the global economic stage.

6. Cultural Diplomacy: Independence provides Scotland with the freedom to engage in cultural diplomacy independently. This involves promoting Scottish arts, heritage, and language on the global stage, fostering international understanding and appreciation for Scotland's rich cultural identity.

7. Human Rights Advocacy:
An autonomous Scotland can actively engage in human rights advocacy at the international level. This includes participating in discussions on human rights violations, supporting initiatives to protect vulnerable populations, and contributing to the advancement of global human rights standards.

8. Health and Education Collaboration:
Independence enables Scotland to directly collaborate with international partners on health and education initiatives. Scotland can contribute expertise, share best practices, and participate in global efforts to address

public health challenges and advance education worldwide.

9. Humanitarian Aid Contribution:
Scotland, as an independent nation, can make direct contributions to international humanitarian aid efforts. This includes participating in relief operations, providing assistance to countries in need, and playing an active role in global responses to humanitarian crises.

10. Representation in Regional Organizations:
Autonomy allows Scotland to seek direct representation in regional organizations. This includes participating in regional forums, addressing regional challenges, and collaborating with neighboring

countries to promote regional stability and development.

11. Participation in Peacekeeping Missions:
Independence provides the opportunity for Scotland to contribute directly to international peacekeeping efforts. This includes deploying peacekeeping forces, participating in conflict resolution initiatives, and contributing to global efforts to maintain peace and security.

In summary, the argument for direct representation in international organizations within the context of Scottish independence emphasizes the potential for Scotland to assert its own voice, priorities, and values on the global stage. Proponents contend that this autonomy enhances Scotland's ability to actively contribute to global governance, diplomacy, and collaborative efforts aimed at addressing shared challenges and building a more interconnected world.

21

Agricultural Autonomy: Cultivating a Tailored Future for Scottish Agriculture

A pivotal argument in favor of Scottish independence lies in the prospect of crafting a bespoke approach to agricultural practices and subsidies. Proponents assert that this autonomy allows Scotland to design policies that address the specific needs of its agricultural sector, promote sustainable practices, and ensure the vitality of rural communities.

1. Tailored Subsidies for Scottish Farmers:
Independence enables Scotland to design agricultural subsidy programs that are customized to the unique challenges faced by its farmers. This includes subsidies that support sustainable farming practices, enhance rural development, and address specific regional needs.

2. Sustainable Agricultural Practices:
An autonomous Scotland can prioritize and incentivize sustainable agricultural practices. Policies can be crafted to support environmentally friendly farming methods, conservation initiatives, and the adoption of technologies that enhance both

productivity and environmental stewardship.

3. Regional Specificities in Crop and Livestock Management: Independence provides the flexibility to address regional specificities in crop and livestock management. Policies can be tailored to the diverse landscapes and climates across Scotland, ensuring that agricultural practices are well-suited to local conditions.

4. Diversification Support: Scotland, as an independent nation, can actively support agricultural diversification. Policies can be designed to encourage farmers to explore alternative crops, value-added products, and agri-tourism, fostering economic resilience and innovation within the sector.

5. Access to Global Markets:
Autonomy allows Scotland to independently negotiate trade agreements that benefit its agricultural sector. This includes securing favorable market access for Scottish agricultural products and ensuring that trade policies align with the interests of Scottish farmers.

6. Innovation and Technology Adoption:
Independence empowers Scotland to promote innovation and technology adoption in agriculture. Policies can incentivize the use of precision farming, smart technologies, and other innovations that enhance productivity

while minimizing environmental impact.

7. Rural Infrastructure Investment:
An autonomous Scotland can strategically invest in rural infrastructure. Policies can focus on improving transportation networks, enhancing access to markets, and providing the necessary support for the overall development of rural communities associated with agriculture.

8. Conservation and Biodiversity Protection:
Independence provides the opportunity to strengthen policies related to conservation and biodiversity protection. Scotland can design agricultural practices that contribute to

preserving natural habitats, protecting wildlife, and promoting biodiversity within farming landscapes.

9. Disaster Resilience and Risk Management:
Scotland, as an independent entity, can design policies to enhance disaster resilience and risk management in agriculture. This includes strategies to address the impacts of extreme weather events, diseases, and other risks that may affect the agricultural sector.

10. Local Food Initiatives:
Autonomy allows for the promotion of local food initiatives. Policies can be crafted to support the production and consumption of locally sourced agricultural products, fostering a sense of community, and ensuring food security at the regional level.

11. Farmer Engagement and Representation:
Independence enables Scotland to enhance farmer engagement and representation in policy-making. Policies can be designed to ensure that the voices of farmers are actively heard and considered, creating a more participatory and responsive agricultural policy framework.

In conclusion, the argument for agricultural autonomy within the context of Scottish independence emphasizes the potential to cultivate a future where policies are tailored to the needs of Scottish farmers and the unique characteristics of the agricultural sector. Proponents contend that this independence allows for a more sustainable, resilient, and innovative approach to agriculture, contributing to the prosperity of rural communities and the overall well-being of the nation.

22

Fisheries Autonomy: Navigating Scotland's Waters with Tailored Policies

A compelling argument for Scottish independence centers around the direct control over fisheries policies, allowing for a bespoke approach that caters to the needs and priorities of Scottish fishermen. Proponents assert that this autonomy empowers Scotland to manage its rich marine resources sustainably, support coastal communities, and shape a thriving and responsible fishing industry.

1. Sustainable Fisheries Practices: Independence provides Scotland the flexibility to design and implement sustainable fisheries practices. Policies can be crafted to ensure responsible harvesting, protect vulnerable species, and maintain the health of marine ecosystems for the long-term benefit of both fishermen and the environment.

2. Tailored Quota Management: An autonomous Scotland can establish quota management systems that are tailored to the specific conditions of its waters. This includes setting quotas based on scientific evidence, ensuring fair distribution, and adapting to the dynamic nature of fish stocks in Scottish seas.

3. Responsive Regulatory Framework:
Independence allows Scotland to develop a responsive regulatory framework for fisheries. Policies can be designed to adapt quickly to changes in fish populations, environmental conditions, and emerging challenges, ensuring the industry remains sustainable and resilient.

4. Support for Small-Scale Fisheries:
Autonomy in fisheries management enables targeted support for small-scale and artisanal fishermen. Policies can be crafted to address the unique needs of smaller vessels, promoting the viability of these operations and preserving the cultural heritage

associated with traditional fishing practices.

5. Community-Based Management Initiatives:
An independent Scotland can promote community-based fisheries management initiatives. Policies can empower local communities to actively participate in decision-making processes, fostering a sense of stewardship and ensuring that fishing practices align with the interests of coastal communities.

6. Scientific Research Collaboration:
Independence provides the opportunity for Scotland to engage in international scientific research collaborations. Policies can support partnerships with research institutions to enhance

understanding of marine ecosystems, fish behavior, and the impacts of climate change on fisheries.

7. Fleet Modernization Support:
Autonomy allows for targeted support for fleet modernization. Policies can be designed to incentivize the adoption of sustainable and technologically advanced fishing practices, ensuring that the Scottish fishing fleet remains competitive on the global stage.

8. Real-Time Monitoring and Surveillance:
An autonomous Scotland can invest in real-time monitoring and surveillance of fisheries activities. Policies can promote the use of technology to track vessels, monitor compliance with regulations, and combat illegal,

unreported, and unregulated (IUU) fishing.

9. Adaptive Response to Climate Change:
Independence empowers Scotland to develop adaptive responses to the impacts of climate change on fisheries. Policies can be crafted to address shifts in fish distribution, changing ocean temperatures, and other climate-related factors that affect the sustainability of the fishing industry.

10. International Fisheries Cooperation:
Autonomy allows Scotland to engage directly in international fisheries cooperation. Policies can be designed to negotiate agreements with neighboring countries, ensuring responsible and sustainable

management of shared fish stocks while protecting the interests of Scottish fishermen.

11. Economic Diversification Strategies:
Independence provides the opportunity to design economic diversification strategies for fishing communities. Policies can support initiatives such as aquaculture, seafood processing, and tourism, creating additional sources of income and reducing reliance solely on fishing.

In conclusion, the argument for fisheries autonomy within the context of Scottish independence emphasizes the potential to navigate Scotland's waters with policies that are finely tuned to the needs of its fishermen and the health of its marine ecosystems.

Proponents contend that this autonomy allows for a more sustainable, adaptive, and community-focused approach to fisheries management, contributing to the resilience and prosperity of Scotland's fishing industry.

23

Crisis Response Autonomy: Navigating Uncertainty with Targeted Policies

A compelling argument for Scottish independence revolves around the capacity to respond swiftly and effectively to economic or public health crises. Proponents assert that this autonomy provides Scotland with the flexibility to design and implement targeted policies that address the specific challenges faced by its economy and public health system during times of uncertainty.

1. Economic Stimulus Tailored to Scottish Needs:
Independence empowers Scotland to implement economic stimulus measures tailored to its unique economic landscape. Policies can be crafted to support industries that are particularly crucial to Scotland's economy, ensuring a rapid and effective response to economic downturns.

2. Adaptive Fiscal Policies:
An autonomous Scotland can develop adaptive fiscal policies to address economic challenges. Policies may include targeted tax incentives, investment in infrastructure projects,

and strategic financial support for businesses, fostering economic resilience and recovery.

3. Public Health Interventions: Independence provides the flexibility to implement public health interventions based on Scotland's specific needs during a crisis. Policies can be designed to address the unique healthcare challenges, allocate resources efficiently, and promote community well-being.

4. Healthcare Capacity Planning: An independent Scotland can engage in strategic healthcare capacity planning. Policies can focus on strengthening the healthcare system, ensuring sufficient hospital beds, medical personnel, and resources are available to respond effectively to public health crises.

5. Social Welfare Support: Autonomy allows Scotland to design social welfare support that responds directly to the social and economic impacts of a crisis. Policies can include targeted financial assistance, unemployment support, and measures to protect vulnerable populations.

6. Industry-Specific Support: Independence empowers Scotland to provide industry-specific support during a crisis. Policies can be crafted to address the unique challenges faced by sectors such as tourism, hospitality, and manufacturing, preserving jobs and ensuring the resilience of critical industries.

7. Rapid Decision-Making:
An autonomous Scotland can make rapid decisions in response to crises. Independence allows for a more streamlined decision-making process, enabling the government to act swiftly in implementing policies and initiatives to address emerging challenges.

8. Customized Economic Recovery Plans:
Autonomy provides the opportunity to develop customized economic recovery plans. Policies can focus on long-term strategies to rebuild and diversify the economy, positioning Scotland for sustained growth and prosperity beyond the immediate crisis.

9. Crisis Communication Strategies:

Independence allows Scotland to implement crisis communication strategies tailored to its population. Policies can focus on transparent communication, building trust, and ensuring that the public is well-informed about the government's actions and recommendations during a crisis.

10. International Collaboration on Crisis Response:
An independent Scotland can engage in international collaboration on crisis response. Policies can facilitate cooperation with other nations, sharing best practices, resources, and expertise to address global challenges, such as pandemics or economic recessions.

11. Agility in Resource Allocation:

Autonomy enables Scotland to allocate resources with agility. During a crisis, policies can be implemented to redirect resources to areas of critical need, ensuring that the government can respond rapidly to evolving circumstances.

In summary, the argument for crisis response autonomy within the context of Scottish independence emphasizes the potential for a nimble and targeted approach to addressing economic or public health crises. Proponents contend that this autonomy allows Scotland to tailor policies to its specific circumstances, fostering resilience, and ensuring the well-being of its citizens during times of uncertainty.

Cultural Diplomacy Autonomy: Showcasing Scotland's Rich Heritage Globally

A compelling aspect of the case for Scottish independence is the opportunity to have independent cultural representation on the global stage. Proponents argue that this autonomy allows Scotland to actively engage in cultural diplomacy, promoting its arts, heritage, and identity worldwide in a way that aligns with its unique values and aspirations.

1. Global Recognition of Scottish Identity:
Independence empowers Scotland to shape its narrative and present its unique identity to the world. Cultural diplomacy allows for the global recognition of Scottish heritage,

fostering a deeper understanding and appreciation of the nation's rich history, traditions, and cultural diversity.

2. Arts and Cultural Exchange Programs:
An autonomous Scotland can design and implement arts and cultural exchange programs with other nations. This facilitates the exchange of ideas, artistic expressions, and cultural practices, contributing to global cultural dialogue and fostering mutual understanding.

3. Promotion of Scottish Arts:
Independence allows Scotland to independently promote its thriving arts scene. Cultural diplomacy policies can spotlight Scottish literature, visual arts, performing arts, and crafts, showcasing

the creativity and talent of Scottish artists to international audiences.

4. Heritage Preservation and Promotion:
An independent Scotland can actively engage in heritage preservation and promotion initiatives. Cultural diplomacy policies can support the conservation of historic sites, artifacts, and traditions, ensuring that Scotland's rich heritage is preserved for future generations and shared with the world.

5. International Cultural Festivals:
Autonomy provides the opportunity to organize and participate in international cultural festivals. Scottish cultural diplomacy can include hosting events that celebrate Scottish music, dance, literature, and cuisine, creating platforms for global audiences to

experience the vibrancy of Scottish culture.

6. Cultural Representation in International Organizations:
Independence enables Scotland to have direct cultural representation in international organizations. This includes participating in UNESCO and other global bodies to advocate for the protection and promotion of cultural heritage and diversity.

7. Collaboration with Global Institutions:
An autonomous Scotland can collaborate with global cultural institutions. Cultural diplomacy policies can facilitate partnerships with renowned museums, galleries, and educational institutions, promoting

Scottish cultural contributions and engaging in collaborative projects.

8. Tourism Promotion through Culture:
Independence allows for the strategic promotion of tourism through cultural diplomacy. Policies can highlight Scotland's cultural attractions, festivals, and events, enticing international visitors to explore the nation's unique cultural offerings.

9. Support for Language and Linguistic Diversity:
Cultural diplomacy can actively support and promote linguistic diversity within Scotland. Policies may include initiatives to preserve and revitalize Scottish languages, ensuring that linguistic heritage plays a central

role in the nation's cultural diplomacy efforts.

10. Film and Media Representation:
Independence provides the platform for independent representation in global film and media. Cultural diplomacy policies can support the creation and promotion of Scottish films, television, and media content, contributing to the global cultural landscape.

11. Educational and Scholarly Exchanges:
Autonomy enables Scotland to initiate educational and scholarly exchanges with global institutions. Cultural diplomacy can include programs that facilitate academic collaborations, research partnerships, and the exchange of knowledge, promoting

Scotland as a hub for intellectual and creative pursuits.

In conclusion, the argument for cultural diplomacy autonomy within the context of Scottish independence emphasizes the potential for Scotland to actively shape its global cultural presence. Proponents contend that this autonomy allows Scotland to share its unique cultural tapestry with the world, fostering international connections, mutual respect, and a deeper appreciation for the diverse contributions of the Scottish people to global culture.

25

Language Preservation Autonomy: Safeguarding the Future of Scottish Gaelic

A crucial aspect of the argument for Scottish independence is the opportunity to have autonomy in language policies, particularly to support and preserve Scottish Gaelic. Proponents argue that this autonomy empowers Scotland to take targeted measures to ensure the vitality, growth, and continued cultural significance of its native languages.

1. Tailored Language Education Programs:
Independence allows Scotland to design and implement language education programs specifically tailored to support and promote Scottish Gaelic. Policies can focus on integrating Gaelic into the education system, providing resources for

language learning, and fostering a multilingual society.

2. Gaelic Media and Broadcasting:
An autonomous Scotland can actively promote the use of Scottish Gaelic in media and broadcasting. Policies may include support for Gaelic-language television, radio, and online content, contributing to the visibility and normalization of the language in everyday life.

3. Community Language Initiatives:
Independence provides the flexibility to support community-led language initiatives. Policies can empower local communities to develop and implement strategies for Gaelic language preservation, ensuring that language

planning is responsive to diverse regional needs.

4. Cultural and Artistic Expression in Gaelic:
An independent Scotland can foster cultural and artistic expression in Scottish Gaelic. Policies may include support for Gaelic literature, poetry, music, and other artistic endeavors, contributing to the richness and diversity of Gaelic cultural heritage.

5. Gaelic Language Technologies:
Autonomy enables Scotland to invest in language technologies that support Scottish Gaelic. Policies can encourage the development of Gaelic language software, online resources, and digital tools to enhance accessibility and usage in the digital age.

6. Incorporation of Gaelic in Public Life:
Independence allows Scotland to actively incorporate Scottish Gaelic into public life. Policies can encourage the use of Gaelic in official documents, signage, and public events, reinforcing the presence of the language as an integral part of national identity.

7. Gaelic Language Standards and Norms:
An autonomous Scotland can set and maintain Gaelic language standards and norms. Policies may include the establishment of language authorities or regulatory bodies to oversee language development, standardization, and the creation of language resources.

8. Integration of Gaelic in Tourism:
Independence provides the opportunity to integrate Scottish Gaelic into tourism initiatives. Policies can encourage the use of Gaelic in tourist information, promotional materials, and cultural experiences, enriching the cultural exchange between visitors and the local community.

9. Collaboration with Gaelic-Speaking Communities:
Autonomy enables Scotland to collaborate directly with Gaelic-speaking communities. Policies can support community-led projects, language revitalization efforts, and initiatives that empower speakers to actively participate in the preservation and promotion of Scottish Gaelic.

10. Recognition of Gaelic as a Working Language:
Independence allows Scotland to recognize Gaelic as a working language in official capacities. Policies can encourage the use of Gaelic in governmental communications, public services, and administrative functions, reinforcing the language's status as a living and evolving part of Scottish culture.

11. International Collaboration for Language Preservation:
Autonomy provides the platform for international collaboration on language preservation. Scotland can engage with other nations facing similar linguistic challenges, sharing best practices and strategies for the preservation and revitalization of minority languages.

In summary, the argument for language preservation autonomy within the context of Scottish independence emphasizes the potential to safeguard the future of Scottish Gaelic. Proponents contend that this autonomy allows Scotland to take decisive steps in ensuring the resilience and vibrancy of its native languages, preserving a crucial aspect of its cultural heritage for generations to come.

26

Tourism Autonomy: Crafting a Distinctive Strategy for Scotland's Unique Appeal

A compelling argument for Scottish independence centers around the opportunity to have autonomy in developing a tourism strategy that aligns seamlessly with Scotland's unique attractions, interests, and cultural richness. Proponents assert that this autonomy enables Scotland to tailor its approach to tourism, showcasing its diverse landscapes, rich history, and vibrant culture to a global audience.

1. Showcasing Natural Landscapes:
Independence empowers Scotland to highlight its natural landscapes and biodiversity. A tourism strategy can focus on sustainable ecotourism, promoting responsible exploration of Scotland's mountains, lochs, and coastal areas while preserving the environmental integrity of these unique spaces.

2. Heritage and Historical Sites:

An autonomous Scotland can strategically promote its heritage and historical sites. Policies may include targeted efforts to showcase castles, ancient ruins, and historical landmarks, providing visitors with immersive experiences that tell the story of Scotland's rich past.

3. Cultural Events and Festivals:
Independence allows Scotland to actively support and promote cultural events and festivals. A tourism strategy can align with the calendar of festivals, such as the Edinburgh Festival Fringe or Highland Games, attracting international visitors and contributing to the cultural vibrancy of the nation.

4. Gastronomic Tourism:
Autonomy provides the opportunity to promote gastronomic tourism. A

tourism strategy can focus on showcasing Scotland's diverse culinary offerings, promoting local and traditional dishes, and positioning Scotland as a destination for food enthusiasts.

5. Adventure Tourism and Outdoor Activities:
An independent Scotland can actively promote adventure tourism and outdoor activities. Policies may include initiatives to support activities such as hiking, mountain biking, and water sports, capitalizing on Scotland's natural playground for adventure enthusiasts.

6. Sustainable Tourism Practices:
Independence empowers Scotland to prioritize sustainable tourism practices. A tourism strategy can include policies

that encourage responsible travel, eco-friendly accommodations, and community engagement, ensuring that tourism contributes positively to local economies and the environment.

7. Cultural Heritage Preservation:
Autonomy allows Scotland to focus on preserving its cultural heritage within the tourism sector. Policies may include measures to protect historic sites, traditional practices, and indigenous languages, ensuring that tourism enhances rather than diminishes cultural authenticity.

8. Film and TV Tourism:
An autonomous Scotland can leverage its cinematic landscapes for film and TV tourism. A tourism strategy can actively promote locations featured in popular films and TV series, attracting

fans and creating economic opportunities for local communities.

9. Accessible Tourism Initiatives: Independence provides the flexibility to develop accessible tourism initiatives. Policies can focus on improving infrastructure, services, and accommodations to ensure that Scotland is welcoming and accessible to visitors of all abilities.

10. Niche Tourism Markets: Independence empowers Scotland to target niche tourism markets. A tourism strategy can identify and cater to specific interests such as wildlife watching, genealogy tourism, or cultural immersion experiences, diversifying the tourism offering.

11. Digital Tourism Promotion:

Autonomy allows Scotland to invest in digital tourism promotion. Policies may include leveraging technology, social media, and online platforms to market Scotland's attractions globally, reaching a diverse and widespread audience of potential visitors.

In conclusion, the argument for tourism autonomy within the context of Scottish independence emphasizes the potential to craft a distinctive strategy that aligns with Scotland's unique appeal. Proponents contend that this autonomy enables Scotland to showcase its authenticity, diversity, and natural beauty, attracting visitors who seek immersive and meaningful experiences in this culturally rich and picturesque nation.

27

Transportation Infrastructure Autonomy: Paving Scotland's Path to Connectivity

A key argument for Scottish independence revolves around the ability to have control over transportation infrastructure development and planning. Proponents assert that this autonomy provides Scotland with the opportunity to shape its own transportation networks, addressing specific regional needs, promoting sustainability, and fostering economic growth.

1. Tailored Regional Connectivity:
Independence empowers Scotland to design transportation infrastructure that caters to the specific connectivity

needs of different regions. Policies can focus on creating efficient links between urban and rural areas, ensuring that transportation networks serve the entire nation.

2. Sustainable and Green Transportation:
An autonomous Scotland can prioritize sustainability in transportation planning. Policies may include investments in green and renewable energy sources for public transport, cycling infrastructure, and initiatives to reduce carbon emissions, contributing to environmental conservation.

3. Integrated Public Transport Systems:
Independence allows for the development of integrated public transport systems. Policies can

encourage seamless connectivity between trains, buses, and other modes of transportation, making it easier for people to move efficiently within and between cities.

4. Strategic Road Network Development:
Autonomy provides the flexibility to plan and develop a strategic road network that aligns with Scotland's economic and geographical considerations. Policies can focus on enhancing major arteries and critical routes, reducing congestion, and improving overall road safety.

5. Investment in Rail Infrastructure:
An independent Scotland can actively invest in rail infrastructure. Policies may include the expansion of rail

networks, upgrading existing lines, and promoting high-speed rail connections, fostering efficient and sustainable transportation options for both passengers and freight.

6. Connectivity to Remote Areas:
Independence empowers Scotland to address connectivity challenges in remote areas. Policies can include targeted investments in transportation infrastructure to link remote communities, enhancing accessibility and supporting economic development in these regions.

7. Infrastructure Resilience and Maintenance:
Autonomy allows for strategic planning and investment in infrastructure resilience and maintenance. Policies can focus on

ensuring the durability of transportation networks, preventing disruptions, and promptly addressing maintenance needs to guarantee long-term functionality.

8. Smart Transportation Technologies:
An autonomous Scotland can embrace smart transportation technologies. Policies may include investments in intelligent transportation systems, data-driven planning, and the integration of technology to enhance the efficiency and safety of transportation networks.

9. Public and Private Collaboration:
Independence provides the opportunity for collaboration between the public and private sectors in transportation development. Policies can encourage

public-private partnerships to leverage expertise, innovation, and funding for infrastructure projects.

10. Active Transportation Promotion:
Autonomy empowers Scotland to actively promote active transportation modes such as walking and cycling. Policies can include the development of pedestrian-friendly infrastructure, cycling lanes, and initiatives to encourage healthier and more sustainable modes of commuting.

11. Adaptation to Future Trends:
Independence allows for adaptability to future transportation trends. Policies can consider emerging technologies, changing travel patterns, and the integration of autonomous vehicles, ensuring that Scotland's transportation

infrastructure remains at the forefront of innovation.

In conclusion, the argument for transportation infrastructure autonomy within the context of Scottish independence emphasizes the potential to shape a comprehensive, sustainable, and resilient network that meets the diverse needs of the nation. Proponents contend that this autonomy enables Scotland to create a transportation system that not only enhances connectivity but also aligns with broader goals of economic development, environmental stewardship, and regional inclusivity.

28

Social Equality Autonomy: Nurturing an Inclusive and Just Scotland

A compelling aspect of the argument for Scottish independence is the opportunity to have autonomy in crafting policies focused on reducing inequality and promoting social justice. Proponents argue that this autonomy empowers Scotland to address its unique social challenges, foster inclusivity, and build a society where all individuals have equal opportunities to thrive.

1. Tailored Social Welfare Programs:
Independence allows Scotland to design and implement social welfare programs that address its specific needs. Policies can focus on supporting

vulnerable populations, addressing poverty, and ensuring that the social safety net is comprehensive and responsive to the diverse needs of the Scottish people.

2. Progressive Taxation Policies: An autonomous Scotland can develop progressive taxation policies. Policies may include measures to ensure that the tax system is fair and equitable, with a focus on redistributing wealth and reducing income inequality.

3. Affordable Housing Initiatives: Independence provides the flexibility to implement affordable housing initiatives. Policies can focus on increasing the supply of affordable housing, promoting mixed-income neighborhoods, and addressing homelessness, ensuring that housing is accessible to all.

4. Education Access and Equality:
Autonomy empowers Scotland to address educational inequalities. Policies may include initiatives to provide equal access to quality education, support for students from disadvantaged backgrounds, and measures to bridge the educational attainment gap.

5. Gender Equality Measures:
An independent Scotland can actively promote gender equality. Policies may include measures to close the gender pay gap, enhance workplace inclusivity, and combat gender-based discrimination, fostering a society where all individuals have equal opportunities regardless of gender.

6. Inclusive Health Policies:
Independence allows for the development of inclusive health policies. Policies can focus on addressing health disparities, ensuring access to healthcare services for all, and promoting public health initiatives that prioritize the well-being of the entire population.

7. Community Empowerment Programs:
Autonomy provides the opportunity for community empowerment programs. Policies can support grassroots initiatives, community-led projects, and participatory decision-making processes, ensuring that local communities have a voice in shaping their own futures.

8. Anti-Discrimination Legislation:
An autonomous Scotland can strengthen anti-discrimination legislation. Policies may include measures to combat racism, xenophobia, homophobia, and other forms of discrimination, fostering a society that values diversity and inclusion.

9. Support for Minority Languages and Cultures:
Independence empowers Scotland to support minority languages and cultures. Policies can include initiatives to preserve and promote languages such as Scottish Gaelic, ensuring that linguistic diversity is celebrated and protected.

10. Disability Inclusion Measures:

Autonomy allows for targeted measures to promote disability inclusion. Policies can focus on improving accessibility, eliminating barriers, and ensuring that individuals with disabilities have equal access to employment, education, and public services.

11. Collaborative Social Partnerships:
Independence provides the opportunity for collaborative social partnerships. Policies may encourage collaboration between government, civil society, and the private sector to collectively address social challenges and promote a more inclusive and just society.

In conclusion, the argument for social equality autonomy within the context of Scottish independence emphasizes the potential to shape a society that prioritizes fairness, inclusivity, and justice for all. Proponents contend that this autonomy enables Scotland to develop policies that are finely tuned to its unique social landscape, fostering a sense of belonging and equal opportunity for every individual in the nation.

29

Local Governance Autonomy: Empowering Regions for Tailored Solutions

A fundamental argument for Scottish independence lies in the opportunity to strengthen local governance structures, allowing for more effective responses to regional variations. Proponents assert that autonomy in local governance empowers communities, fosters regional identity, and enables the implementation of policies that are finely tuned to the unique needs of different areas within Scotland.

1. Devolved Decision-Making Powers:
Independence provides the opportunity for enhanced devolved decision-making powers to local authorities. Policies can empower councils with greater autonomy to make decisions on matters such as education, healthcare, and infrastructure, ensuring that local perspectives are central to policymaking.

2. Tailored Economic Development Strategies:
An autonomous Scotland can support tailored economic development

strategies at the local level. Policies may include initiatives that focus on the unique strengths and challenges of different regions, fostering economic growth and job creation that aligns with the specific needs of local communities.

3. Community-Led Development Projects:
Independence allows for the promotion of community-led development projects. Policies can encourage local communities to actively participate in decision-making processes, propose and implement projects that enhance the quality of life, and contribute to the development of vibrant, self-sustaining communities.

4. Regional Infrastructure Planning:

Autonomy empowers local authorities to engage in regional infrastructure planning. Policies may include initiatives to address specific infrastructure needs of different regions, ensuring that transportation, utilities, and public services are strategically planned to meet local demands.

5. Educational Autonomy for Local Authorities:
An independent Scotland can grant greater autonomy to local authorities in educational matters. Policies may involve devolving decision-making powers to schools and communities, allowing them to shape curricula, teaching methodologies, and educational priorities based on local needs.

6. Healthcare Planning at the Local Level:
Independence provides the opportunity to involve local communities in healthcare planning. Policies can empower local health boards to make decisions that address the unique health challenges of their regions, ensuring that healthcare services are tailored to the needs of local populations.

7. Cultural and Arts Funding for Regions:
Autonomy allows for the allocation of cultural and arts funding to regions. Policies may include initiatives that support regional cultural events, festivals, and artistic endeavors, promoting local creativity and preserving diverse cultural expressions.

8. Sustainable Environmental Policies:
An independent Scotland can engage local communities in the development of sustainable environmental policies. Policies may include initiatives to address regional environmental challenges, promote conservation efforts, and encourage local participation in sustainable practices.

9. Tourism Promotion at the Local Level:
Independence empowers local authorities to actively engage in tourism promotion. Policies can encourage regions to highlight their unique attractions, cultural heritage, and events, fostering tourism that benefits local economies and showcases the distinctiveness of each region.

10. Responsive Social Policies:
Autonomy allows for the tailoring of social policies to address regional variations. Policies may involve local authorities in shaping social welfare programs, healthcare initiatives, and educational support systems that respond directly to the social needs of different communities.

11. Collaborative Regional Planning:
Independence provides the opportunity for collaborative regional planning. Policies can encourage local authorities to work together on cross-cutting issues, fostering cooperation and coordination to address challenges that transcend individual regions.

In conclusion, the argument for local governance autonomy within the context of Scottish independence emphasizes the potential to create a governance framework that is responsive to the diverse needs and aspirations of different regions. Proponents contend that this autonomy empowers communities, fosters local innovation, and contributes to the overall resilience and vibrancy of Scotland as a nation.

30

Digital Infrastructure Autonomy: Navigating Scotland's Technological Future Independently

A compelling argument for Scottish independence centers around the ability to make independent decisions on digital infrastructure investment and expansion. Proponents assert that this autonomy allows Scotland to shape its technological future, foster innovation, and address the unique digital needs of its communities.

1. Broadband Connectivity for All:
Independence provides the opportunity to prioritize universal broadband connectivity. Policies can focus on closing the digital divide by investing in infrastructure projects that ensure high-speed internet access for all regions, urban and rural alike.

2. Rural Digital Inclusion Initiatives:
An autonomous Scotland can actively support digital inclusion in rural areas. Policies may include targeted

initiatives to provide internet access, digital literacy programs, and support for businesses to thrive in remote locations, ensuring equitable access to digital opportunities.

3. Smart City Initiatives:
Independence allows for the development of smart city initiatives. Policies can encourage the integration of digital technologies to enhance urban living, improve efficiency in public services, and create sustainable, technologically advanced urban environments.

4. Innovation Hubs and Tech Clusters:
Autonomy empowers Scotland to establish innovation hubs and tech clusters. Policies may involve investments in research and

development, technology parks, and initiatives that foster collaboration between academia, industry, and startups, driving technological innovation.

5. Digital Skills Training:
An independent Scotland can focus on digital skills training. Policies may include initiatives to equip the workforce with the skills needed for the digital economy, ensuring that individuals have the capabilities to thrive in an increasingly technology-driven world.

6. Cybersecurity Infrastructure:
Independence provides the opportunity to strengthen cybersecurity infrastructure. Policies can focus on investing in robust cybersecurity measures to protect critical

infrastructure, businesses, and individuals from cyber threats and attacks.

7. Open Data Initiatives:
Autonomy allows for the implementation of open data initiatives. Policies can promote transparency and innovation by making government data accessible to the public, businesses, and researchers, fostering the development of data-driven solutions.

8. E-Government Services:
An autonomous Scotland can prioritize the development of e-government services. Policies may include initiatives to digitize public services, streamline administrative processes, and enhance citizen engagement through online platforms, making

government services more accessible and efficient.

9. Digital Healthcare Solutions:
Independence empowers Scotland to invest in digital healthcare solutions. Policies can focus on implementing telehealth services, electronic health records, and other digital innovations to improve healthcare accessibility and delivery across the nation.

10. Data Privacy and Digital Rights:
Autonomy allows for the crafting of robust data privacy and digital rights policies. Policies may involve creating legislation that protects individual privacy, regulates the use of personal data, and ensures that digital rights are safeguarded in the digital age.

11. Sustainable Digital Infrastructure:
Independence provides the flexibility to invest in sustainable digital infrastructure. Policies can include initiatives that prioritize energy-efficient technologies, reduce the environmental impact of digital infrastructure, and contribute to Scotland's overall sustainability goals.

In conclusion, the argument for digital infrastructure autonomy within the context of Scottish independence emphasizes the potential to navigate Scotland's technological future independently. Proponents contend that this autonomy enables Scotland to harness the transformative power of digital technologies for the benefit of its citizens, businesses, and overall economic and social development.

www.ingramcontent.com/pod-product-compliance
Lightning Source LLC
Chambersburg PA
CBHW070931260726
48661CB00003B/926